GET ACTIVE!

WINTER SPORTS

Barbara C. Bourassa

Copyright © QED Publishing 2007

First published in the UK in 2007 by
QED Publishing
A Quarto Group company
226 City Road
London EC1V 2TT
www.qed-publishing.co.uk

A catalogue record for this book is available from the British Library.

ISBN 978 1 84538 649 8

Written by Barbara C. Bourassa
Edited, designed and picture researched by
    Starry Dog Books Ltd
Consultant Steven Downes, of the Sports Journalists'
    Association www.sportsjournalists.co.uk

Publisher Steve Evans
Creative Director Zeta Davies
Senior Editor Hannah Ray

Printed and bound in China

Website information is correct at time of going to press. However, the publishers cannot accept liability for any information or links found on third-party websites.

All the sports in this book involve differing degrees of difficulty and the publisher would strongly advise that none of the activities mentioned is undertaken without adult supervision or the guidance of a professional coach.

Words in **bold** can be found in the Glossary on pages 30–31.

CONTENTS

THE winter sports that are grouped together in this book are usually done in places where there is plenty of snow and ice. Some can be done all year round, such as ice skating (in an indoor **rink**) or downhill skiing (on **artificial snow**), but for the most part the sports are meant to be done outside. Many of them began in countries that are snowy for many months of the year.

The first snowboard, called the snurfer, was developed in the 1960s. The idea came from joining two skis together.

Snow time!

Some winter sports, such as snowboarding and downhill skiing, are especially fun to do just after a heavy snowfall! Skating and ice hockey, of course, require ice. And while cross-country skiing and snowmobiling can be done on just a few centimetres of snow, both are more fun if there is a solid base of snow underfoot.

REMEMBER TO TAKE IT SLOWLY!

Before you take up any new sport, it is important to remember that the **professionals** you may watch performing on television – for instance ski jumping or playing ice hockey – are very experienced and most of them have been practising for years. So don't expect to be able to do the same moves that they can, or go as fast as they do, without first learning the basics of your chosen sport.

Safety first

You'll notice that most children who you see snowboarding, downhill skiing or playing ice hockey wear helmets. These provide essential protection for the head if you fall at high speed or onto hard ice. Ice hockey also requires lots of body padding for protection against flying **pucks**, raised sticks and other players! Different sports need different gear, and wearing the right protective gear for your winter sport will help to keep you safe while you have fun!

Coaching tips

As any good **coach** will tell you, learning a new sport means understanding and mastering the basic skills, looking after your equipment properly and doing lots of practice. All winter sports, from sledging to ski jumping, are part of a healthy and active lifestyle, so remember to drink plenty of water, eat well and take breaks whenever you need to, whether you're playing in an ice hockey game or cross-country skiing along **trails** through the woods.

SNOWBOARDING is a relatively new sport. It involves riding a specially designed board down a snow-covered hill or mountain. Since becoming an Olympic sport, it has become much more popular.

Riding the board

A snowboard is larger than a **skateboard**, but smaller than a **surfboard**. To ride the board, you stand on it sideways wearing snowboard boots, which fit into **bindings** that hold the boots to the board. Snowboarders wear all the usual warm winter gear – snow trousers, warm coat, gloves – and often goggles to protect their eyes from the glare of the sun.

REACHING THE TOP

To get up big hills, such as those found at snowboard or ski resorts, snowboarders use a lift. On some, you stand on your board while the lift pulls you up the hill. On others, you sit in a chair (a chairlift, above) or ride in a gondola (an enclosed cabin) to be carried up the hill.

If you are just learning to snowboard, holding your arms out to the sides will help you to balance.

Sense of balance

Snowboarding requires good balance. You need to be able to shift your weight to stay upright as you move along, especially when you go fast. When you first learn snowboarding, you'll probably fall down quite often – this is quite normal! But your **muscles** will soon get the hang of riding downhill.

To learn more about snowboarding, check out this website: www.abc-of-snowboarding.com

BOARD AND BOOTS

Professional snowboarders generally wear hard boots, a bit like downhill ski boots. Some professionals prefer to use an Alpine snowboard, which is stiffer and narrower than a normal board.

Starting out

If you want to try snowboarding, you could buy a simple board that can be used with standard winter boots. Instead of placing your feet into bindings, you slide the front of your boot under a loop-like device. This type of snowboard is great for beginners, because if you lose your balance and fall over, your feet just fall out of the loops.

▶ *Snowboarding is very popular with young people. From age 15 upwards, both boys and girls can take part in the Winter Olympics.*

WORLD RECORD

According to the Guinness Book of World Records, Karine Ruby of France has won a record 11 women's World Cup snowboarding titles.

Where to snowboard

Anywhere that's suitable for skiing or sledging is also suitable for snowboarding. But be sure to watch out for other children and trees that might be in your path! More advanced snowboarders can visit a snowboard park (also called a terrain park). Some terrain parks are stand-alone, meaning they are only designed for snowboarders. Others are part of a larger resort that has trails and areas for both downhill skiers and snowboarders on the same mountain.

Terrain park obstacles

Terrain parks have small hills or bumps that more experienced snowboarders ride or jump over, as well as rails for sliding down. In an event called snowboard cross, snowboarders race down a steep course, and the fastest snowboarder wins!

▶ *To slide down a terrain park rail, you need to have excellent balance and plenty of experience.*

SNOWBOARD LINGO
Like surfing, snowboarding has a language all of its own. The terms vary depending on where you're snowboarding. In the USA, to 'roll down the windows' means to swing your arms wildly in the air in an attempt to recover your balance, while 'huckers' are snowboarders who fling themselves through the air, but don't land on their feet.

International champions

At the 2006 Winter Olympics in Turin, northern Italy, many of the snowboarders who won medals came, not surprisingly, from snowy countries. They included Philip Schoch of Sweden; Paul-Henri Delerue of France; Amelie Kober of Germany; and Dominique Maltais of Canada.

Half pipe

Professional snowboarders compete in various kinds of competitions. One takes place on a feature called a half pipe – a long, smooth channel in the snow that looks like a tube that's been cut in half lengthways. In the men's and women's half-pipe event, experienced snowboarders perform jumps, flips and other fancy moves along the edge of the half pipe, or inside it.

The Alley Oop trick is only for the most experienced snowboarders. It involves doing a 180 degree turn in mid air above the lip, or top edge, of the half pipe.

OWNHILL skiing (also called Alpine skiing) is a fun sport for boys and girls. The aim is to ride your skis downhill, making turns, going over small bumps and feeling the wind in your face. When you ski, you balance yourself on the two skis and try to keep them next to each other and pointing in the right direction. This can take some practice, so don't be surprised if you fall over a few times!

EQUIPMENT

To try downhill skiing, you'll need a pair of skis and some ski boots, which attach to the skis with metal bindings. It's also helpful to have two poles to help push yourself along or steer your way downhill. For warmth and safety, it's best to wear a padded ski coat and ski trousers, a hat, gloves, a helmet and eye protection, such as goggles or sunglasses.

For young skiers like this three-year-old, a moving carpet is a great way to be carried up a slight slope.

Going up!

If you are skiing at a mountain ski resort, you will probably take a lift up the mountain. On some lifts, you keep your skis on and the lift pulls or carries you up the hill. If you ride in a gondola (an enclosed cabin) you take your skis off and sit or stand for the ride up the mountain. Some ski resorts have a 'moving carpet' – a large, flat **conveyor belt** that carries you up a slope with your skis on. At the top, you step off the moving carpet and ski back down the hill.

Gentle slopes

If you are a beginner, you will probably learn to ski on a gently sloping hill (called a nursery slope), where you can get used to the feeling of wearing ski boots and moving around on the snow on skis. As you progress, you can move to a steeper hill with a **piste**.

DID YOU KNOW?

Mountain ranges all over the world have been developed for downhill skiing. Among the most famous are the Swiss Alps (in Switzerland), where you can find ski resorts such as Davos, St Moritz and Wengen. There are other famous ski resorts in the Andes – the long mountain range that runs down the west coast of South America – as well as in the USA and Canada.

▲ Most skiers wear sunglasses to protect their eyes against the sunshine reflecting off the snow, or goggles to protect their eyes against wind and snow.

Olympic events

Downhill skiing is fun to do, but it's also very exciting to watch! The Winter Olympics feature a number of different events that involve downhill skiing. Some are races, where the skiers try to ski down the mountain as fast as they can. In other events, the skiers are judged on their ability to ski over bumps (called **moguls**) or perform difficult manoeuvres (freestyle).

Races

There are many different kinds of downhill ski races. In a **slalom** race, skiers race downhill making tight turns around a set of skinny, flexible poles called slalom poles, which are stuck in the snow along the track. The skier who skis down the course fastest without missing out any of the poles wins the race. The skiers wear special padding on their legs and arms in case they hit the poles as they fly by.

Freestyle

In a freestyle, or **aerial**, skiing event, the skier skis down a ramp that sends him or her up into the air. The skier then has three or four seconds to perform manoeuvres such as flips, twists and spirals. Judges look for how neatly the skier lands, as well as the difficulty of the manoeuvres performed in the air.

26
ST.MORITZ
Audi

⬧ *The Olympic 'combined' event includes one downhill and two slalom runs in a day.*

SKI RESCUE

If a skier at a resort falls and gets hurt, he or she may be rescued by the ski patrol. These experienced skiers ski all over the mountains during the day, keeping a look out for people who need help. Sometimes helicopters are used to rescue skiers from the tallest mountains.

ARTIFICIAL SNOW

Ski resorts that don't get enough real snow may use snow machines and blowers to make artificial snow.

Downhill

In an event called the downhill, skiers race one at a time down a long, steep, winding course as fast as they can. The skier who gets to the bottom in the quickest time is the winner. Downhill racers wear padded ski outfits, which fit very close to their bodies in order to make them more **aerodynamic**. The pads, as well as their helmets, protect them in case they should fall.

Tina Maze of Slovakia speeds downhill during an Alpine Ski World Cup Women's Super-G race in St Moritz (January 2006). Maze finished in second place.

SKATING is a fun sport in which you wear ice skates – boots with sharp blades on the bottom – to move quickly across ice. People skate on frozen ponds or lakes in winter, or on indoor or outdoor skating rinks. Some people skate just for fun! Others master all kinds of difficult manoeuvres, which they perform in front of judges in skating competitions.

SKATE FACTS

Skaters can choose different types of skate depending on their skill or the kind of skating they want to do. (Check out www.isu.org for information about different kinds of skating.) Beginners can wear simple recreational skates, while professional skaters may have skates specially made to fit their feet.

Figure skating

In **figure skating** competitions, skaters perform twirls, flips and jumps, usually in time to music. Figure skaters at the Winter Olympics are judged on how well they perform their manoeuvres, how difficult the moves are and how well they skate with their partners. There are singles competitions for solo men and women skaters, as well as pairs skating (for a man and woman partnership) and ice dancing.

◀ *In this figure skating move, called a death spiral, the boy holds the girl's hand and pulls her in a circle around him.*

Balancing act

Skating requires good balance – after all, you need to balance the weight of your entire body on two very thin pieces of metal. If you are a beginner, you should expect to fall down frequently! You may also get sore ankles, because your ankles will have to work hard to keep your feet at the right angles.

SKATING SAFETY

Never skate on a frozen lake, pond, river or stream that has not first been checked for safety by an adult. While the ice may look thick enough to skate on, in reality it may not be strong enough to take your weight. Streams can be particularly dangerous, because the water moving under the ice may prevent the ice from freezing completely. It's always safer to skate on a rink.

▲ *These young boys are having a friendly speed-skating race. Speed skating is also an exciting Winter Olympic sport, in which skaters race around an oval-shaped rink.*

DID YOU KNOW?

The special machine that cleans the ice at a skating rink is called a Zamboni. It is named after Frank Zamboni, its inventor.

ONCE YOU know how to skate, you may want to learn how to play ice hockey. Ice hockey is a fast-paced, exciting game similar to field hockey, but played on ice with special sticks and a puck instead of a ball. A puck is a hard, smooth disc that glides easily across the ice. The aim is to hit the puck into the goal more often than the other team. The team with the most goals wins.

The stick

An ice hockey stick has a straightish end (about 25cm long) for hitting the puck. Some ice hockey players wrap black tape around the ends of their sticks to give them better grip on the puck.

OLYMPIC RIVALS

Ice hockey is a popular Winter Olympic sport. Rivalry between the cold-weather nations of Finland, the USA, Russia (above, in red, playing Slovakia) and Norway is legendary. At the 2006 Winter Olympics in Italy, Sweden won the men's gold medal, while Canada won the women's event.

➤ *In ice hockey, the referee wears skates, too, both to keep up with the action and to stay out of the way!*

Game basics

There may be up to 22 players in an ice hockey team, but only six play on the ice at one time. One of them is the goalkeeper, two play in **defence**, and there are three **attackers**. The action is so fast-paced that player changes may happen every few minutes. The area of play is called the rink, and is marked with coloured lines painted beneath the ice.

KEEP SAFE

Ice hockey players hit the puck very hard, which can cause it to fly into the air. If you've ever watched an ice hockey game, you may have noticed the clear, reinforced-plastic partitions that separate the fans from the players. These are designed to prevent pucks from flying into the crowd.

EQUIPMENT

To play ice hockey, you'll need skates; a hockey helmet (often with a cage across the front to protect the face); gloves; shin, shoulder and elbow pads; waterproof trousers; and a stick. For information about all things to do with ice hockey, check out: www2.nhl.com/kids

DID YOU KNOW?

If an ice hockey player breaks the rules, he or she may be sent to the **penalty box** to sit out the action for a short time.

⬆ *With his wide leg pads, the goalkeeper blocks much of the goal when he stands in front of it. The forward has to aim carefully before striking the puck.*

SLEDGING is probably the easiest winter sport to try – all you need is a snow-covered hill and a sledge of some kind.

Sledge types

Sledges come in many shapes and sizes. On an old-fashioned toboggan, several people can sit together, one behind the other. A flying saucer, on the other hand, is meant for just one person. It resembles cartoon drawings of **UFO**s from outer space!

DOG SLEDGE RACE
In Alaska, sledges pulled by teams of dogs compete in the Iditarod Trail **Sled** Dog Race. Competitors in this annual race travel more than 1000 miles over snow and ice.

Look out below!

The first place you are likely to try sledging is in your garden (if it has a slope!), in a park or on a field. The hill needn't be big, but it's important that you can see the bottom from the top, so you don't bump into anything on the way down. (You'll need to ask permission if you want to sledge on someone else's property.)

◄ Many modern sledges, like this flying saucer, are made of plastic and have handles to hold on to.

Keeping warm

You'll need to dress in warm winter gear for sledging: thick trousers, a coat, mittens or gloves and a hat (or helmet). Don't forget to take a thermos flask full of hot chocolate to warm you up, and a snack, to give you energy to walk back up the hill.

SLEDGING WITHOUT SNOW

Just because some people live in parts of the world where there isn't much snow, doesn't mean they can't enjoy sledging! On the islands of Hawaii, young boys ride banana tree stumps down grassy hills. For an extreme version of sledging, the ancient Hawaiians rode wooden sledges down hills of hardened **lava**.

◄ This toboggan has two runners with a raised seat in between. The front rider holds on to the sledge, and the second rider holds on to the person in front.

IF YOU LIKE sledging, you may also like watching sports that involve sledges. At the Winter Olympics there are several events in which athletes ride a sledge-like device down a hill, usually at very high speeds. The sledges have some unusual names: there's the two- or four-person **bobsleigh**, the **luge** and the **skeleton**.

Fearless and fast

In the skeleton event, one person lies on a small sledge and rides head first down an ice track. The aim is to reach the bottom in a faster time than the other competitors. In the luge competition, one or two riders lie on their backs on the luge and speed down the track feet first. The riders grip handles on the edge of the luge, which helps them to steer.

▶ *Maya Pederson of Switzerland speeds down the track during her first run at the 2006 Skeleton World Cup in Switzerland.*

SNOW TUBING

If you are attracted to the idea of bobsleighing, a good place to start might be with a very fast form of sledging called snow tubing. A snow tube is an inflated rubber ring that you sit on. The air provides a cushion between you and the ground, so the ride doesn't feel too bumpy! The tube moves so fast because it's very light.

WHAT TO WEAR

All bobsleigh, luge and skeleton athletes wear helmets to protect their heads and faces. They also wear tight racing suits (often brightly coloured) to make their bodies more aerodynamic.

At the start of a four-man bobsleigh race, the teammates reach a speed of about 40kph before they jump on board.

Bobsleighing

In the bobsleigh event, two or four riders sit one behind the other in a specially designed sledge.

At the start of the race, the teammates push the bobsleigh to get it moving and then leap on and sit down. The bobsleigh races down a narrow, high-banked, twisting ice track, usually about 1200m to 1400m long, at speeds of up to 130kph. The team that makes it to the bottom in the fastest time wins!

CROSS-COUNTRY skiing is just what it sounds like: wearing a pair of skis to travel across country (rather than down a hill). You use two poles for balance and to help push yourself along. Trails or tracks for cross-country skiers may wind through woods and across frozen lakes and fields, taking you through beautiful countryside. Classic-style cross-country skiing is a hobby sport, while professional skiers compete in races.

Classic style

The classic style of cross-country skiing is the easiest to learn. You place your skis side by side, about 15cm apart, then slide one foot forward at a time, as if you were walking without taking your feet off the ground. Gradually the walking action will turn into skiing.

WHERE TO SKI

In some parts of the world, such as the USA, Canada and northern Europe, you can ski on special trails – wide, flat areas of snow that have been prepared for easy skiing. Some people prefer to make their own trail, forging a path across wilderness countryside (above), and then spend the night in a tent. Brrr! Don't forget to ask permission if you want to ski across someone else's property.

Good exercise

Cross-country skiing is very good exercise, as it uses many of the big muscles in your body, including your arms and legs. Most cross-country skiers don't wear big, bulky winter gear, but instead wrap up in several layers of warm clothing that can be removed (or put back on) as the body heats up (or cools down).

↑ If you are a beginner at cross-country skiing, you can use the poles to help yourself balance and prevent a fall.

SKIS

For cross-country skiing you will need a pair of cross-country skis – which are very long and narrow – a pair of boots and some poles. The boots are attached to the skis, but generally only at the toes, letting the backs of the boots lift up as you move along.

DID YOU KNOW?

In Finland during the **Winter War** of 1939, some of the Finnish army wore cross-country skis while fighting the Russians.

◀ Many people cross-country ski in winter along paths that are used for hiking in the summer. If you are planning an expedition, don't forget to carry food and drink to help give you energy.

Racing for professionals

At the professional level, there are several types of cross-country ski races. In some events, skiers use the classic style of skiing; in others they 'skate' along the snow (moving their skis from side to side in order to go faster).

The biathlon race

Cross-country skiing may date to prehistoric times, when some people wore skis to hunt animals. This may explain the winter sport of biathlon, which combines cross-country skiing with rifle shooting. Competitors stop two or four times during the race at a shooting range, where they fire a round of shots – sometimes from standing, sometimes lying down. The aim is to hit five targets with five bullets. There are various penalties for missing the targets.

DID YOU KNOW?

Skijoring is a sport that combines cross-country skiing with dogs (or sometimes horses). The skier is pulled along by the dogs.

Junior races

In northern Europe and Canada, children compete in the same types of cross-country ski races as the adults. In a sprint-style race, you ski as fast as you can from one point to another. In the pursuit race, you start out doing one style of skiing (such as classic – sliding one foot forward and then the other), then stop halfway through the race, change to a second set of skis, and finish the race using the freestyle, or skating, style of cross-country skiing.

◄ *Competitors in cross-country ski races, like these children in Oslo, Norway, wear numbered bibs so the judges know who's who.*

In snowshoeing, you clomp through the snow wearing large, oval snowshoes. Old-fashioned ones were made of wood and string, and resembled tennis racquets; modern ones are made of lightweight metal and plastic.

Long-distance and relay races

Sweden has a race called the Vasaloppet, in which athletes ski for 90km. It is considered by some to be the longest, oldest and biggest cross-country ski race in the world. In contrast, in ski relay races, four skiers in a team each complete a distance of 10km for men and 5km for women. The team whose fourth skier completes the course first wins!

▶ *A competitor in the women's 4x5km relay race at the cross-country skiing World Cup. In a relay, skiers take turns on the course.*

25

SKI JUMPING is a specialized sport performed in competitions by highly experienced athletes. The skier skis down a long, steep slope with knees bent and their body close to the skis. This helps build up speed. From a ramp at the bottom, he or she launches into the air and leans forwards so his or her body is almost in line with the skis. After sailing through the air, the skier lands far down the hill. Points are scored for distance, with extra points given for style and form. The ski jumper with the most points wins.

Three styles

At the professional level, there are three ski jumping events: normal hill, large hill and team events. The best ski jumpers reach distances of 90 to 100m off the normal hill, and fly through the air for 115 to 130m off the large hill.

SKI JUMPING EQUIPMENT

The skis used in ski jumping are longer and wider than those used in downhill or cross-country skiing. The shape of the skis helps the jumper sail through the air. Professional ski jumpers wear close-fitting suits and helmets to protect their heads in case they fall.

➡ *From the top of this hill, the ski jumper can see the ramp at the bottom and the ski resort of Lillehammer, Norway, in the distance.*

Start small!

Ski jumping is a great sport to watch live or on televison. However, if you really want to have a go, first you need to learn how to ski downhill, and then how to do small jumps. Gradually, with lots of practice and the help of a coach, you can build up to doing bigger jumps.

Practising on small hills is a good way to get the feel of flying through the air.

CANADIAN CHAMPION

Fourteen-year-old Trevor Morrice of Canada won the 2006 North American Junior Ski Jumping Championships. Trevor finished with 246.5 points on the K90 hill. The term K90 refers to the distance between where the skier leaves the jump (the takeoff) and the part of the hill where it starts to flatten out (called the **K point**, or critical point). On a normal hill the distance is 90m — hence the name K90.

A SNOWMOBILE is a motorized sledge driven by a petrol engine. It has one central, rubber **caterpillar track**, and skis instead of wheels. To drive it, you sit on the back as you would on a motorbike. Snowmobile racing is popular in the USA. People race snowmobiles downhill, across country and around oval ice tracks.

SLEIGH RIDING

Before the snowmobile was invented, people in snowy places often travelled by horse-drawn sleigh. Today, sleigh riding is a popular tourist activity in ski resorts and towns in snowy countries, such as Russia.

Iron Dog

The longest, toughest snowmobile race in the world takes place in Alaska, USA, and is called the Iron Dog. Competitors race over a distance of 3172km.

Snow cats

Snow cats are large snow vehicles used for 'grooming' ski trails. Running on caterpillar tracks, they pull along a bar-shaped device that flattens or smooths out the snow.

*Some snow cats are used on ski mountains, while others are used to transport people or goods in snowy parts of the world, or for exploring the **Arctic** region.*

Take it carefully!

If you want to try snowmobiling, you'll need warm-weather gear – thick trousers, a warm coat, gloves and boots – as well as a helmet. Some snowmobiles are designed for two people – the passenger sits behind the driver and holds onto two side handles. Snowmobiles can go very fast, but unless you are experienced, it's best to keep your speed down and to always have adult supervision.

◀ *The sport of snowmobiling is best done in good weather conditions, when you can clearly see the trail ahead of you.*

SURVIVING THE WINTER

In some parts of the world, such as in the Arctic, snowmobiles and snow cats are an important means of transportation. Many people depend on them for survival, especially during the long winter months when thick snow covers the land.

aerial A style of downhill skiing in which skiers perform jumps, flips, twists and other moves.

aerodynamic Something with a streamlined shape that allows wind or air to flow over it easily, making it go faster.

Arctic The icy region around the North Pole.

artificial snow Snow made by a machine such as a blower.

attacker A player who tries to score goals in the opposing team's goal.

bindings Devices that hold boots to skis or a snowboard. Downhill skiers insert their boots toe-first into the bindings, then put their heels down to snap the bindings closed around the boots. Snowboarders place their whole boots into the bindings, which have straps over the toes and ankles that they tighten by hand.

bobsleigh A long fibreglass or metal sledge, with two sets of steel runners, big enough for two or four athletes to sit inside.

boogie board A smaller, shorter version of a surfboard, used in shallow waters.

caterpillar track A steel band looped around the wheels of a vehicle such as a snow cat. It allows the vehicle to travel over rough ground or across snow and ice.

coach An instructor or trainer who helps players improve their skills.

conveyor belt A continuous moving band on which people stand to move from one place to another.

defence A player or players who defend their own goal and try to stop the other team scoring.

figure skating Performing moves such as jumps or spins on ice to music, either alone or with a partner.

K point The distance to aim for when ski jumping, marked by the K line on the landing strip. For a normal hill (see page 26), the K point is 90m, and for a large hill it is 120m.

lava Hot, semi-fluid volcanic rock.

luge A type of sledge with two runners, called steels, and a flat seat on which the rider lies down.

mogul A steep mound or ridge of snow on a ski slope.

muscles Tissue in the body that controls the movement of all our body parts (including legs and arms).

penalty box A place where ice hockey players sit out play if they have broken the rules.

piste A downhill ski run.

professional A person who is paid to play a sport.

puck In ice hockey, a small, thick disc that players try to hit into the goals. Made of smooth rubber, it glides easily across the ice.

rink A frozen surface for ice hockey or skating, kept frozen by machines.

skateboard A board measuring about 75cm long and about 20cm wide with two wheels at each end.

skeleton A type of racing sledge with two runners and a steel frame. Riders speed headfirst down a curving, icy track at up to 145kph.

slalom A race course with obstacles that competitors must zigzag around.

sled The American term for sledge.

surfboard A long, flat board about 2.7m long and 0.6m wide, used for riding the waves at sea.

trail The path that a snowboarder or skier follows down a mountain, and that a cross-country skier follows through the countryside.

UFO The letters stand for Unidentified Flying Object.

Winter War A short war between the former Soviet Union and Finland, (1939–1940).

WEBSITES
Snowboarding: www.abc-of-snowboarding.com
Skating: www.isu.org/
Ice hockey: www2.nhl.com/kids